The One Pound
Challenge

ONE
POUND
CHALLENGE

The Ultimate Entrepreneurial
Business Adventure

Alan Radbourne

Contents

Dedication to inspiration - 23/04/14

'I dedicate this book to inspiration in my personal life, work life and faith life. This book will contain insight into that which has inspired me, challenged me and just tickled my interest throughout this business adventure.

I've chosen this beginning as I'm sat in a simple yet effective (much like myself) camping pod on the Llyn Peninsula in North Wales looking out across the vast sea expanse, a great place to begin my journey of inspiration.

As I sit here with just five weeks remaining of my One Pound Challenge, I feel it is right to begin to put pen to paper to explain this business adventure that I've been on over the last year. I hope that this book will inspire and encourage people to step out in their own businesses, to manage their finances better, or just to act as an exceptionally good table leg prop to stop a wobbly table.'

This was the first note I made when I began to recall my year to create this book. It has focused my thoughts and motivated me to continue writing. I hope the dedication to inspiration will be evident as you read about my journey.

Part 1: Introduction

ONE
POUND
CHALLENGE

1. Introduction

This book isn't a self-help or how-to book. It does not give business theory or claim to have all the answers. It is not trying to reinvent the wheel or sell you a product.

This book is a story. A real-life, stripped-down and honest story of a graduate's journey into the world of work through a year long adventure that challenges the perceptions of what it takes to start a business.

Welcome to the One Pound Challenge: A Business Adventure from a £1 Investment!

I am Alan Radbourne. A Loughborough University graduate in Geography and Sport Science, which apparently qualifies me for running and colouring in at the same time!

Before we begin, I would like to make clear that this book isn't based on academic theory, because I have never studied business before. So I am, quite possibly like you, a complete business novice.

Don't let that change your mind about this book. Give the story a chance. The lack of my formal business education or training, I think, only enriches the possibility of my story being your story. This journey relies upon the real life experience of stepping out and trying something new. Don't we all wonder what stepping out might look like in our own story?

About the One Pound Challenge

The One Pound Challenge was a business adventure to see what could be achieved from only a £1 investment and in one year. It was a year for me to work full time to invest and reinvest in a variety of self-led projects. Could I turn a £1 investment into my first graduate salary?

Throughout the year I chose to not take any money out of the challenge, but instead to continually find ways to reinvest every penny I'd made to accurately see what really could be achieved from something as little as a £1 coin.

After a year of hard work, countless ups and downs and more project ideas than I could handle, my £1 investment had grown to a little over £20,000 gross profit with an income of around £38,000.

Still, the purpose of the challenge was to do far more than tide me over in my graduate year and avoid the daily grind of finding what some might call a *'real job'*. I wanted the story of my journey to inspire and encourage people from the initial idea of the challenge. I wanted people to know that there are always options to take hold of your finances; there are ways to earn extra cash, to stay out of debt and that no one needs a gigantic business investment to get their dream business off the ground. Having started from £1, it demonstrates that everyone can access their financial freedom and their business dreams. Everyone has the potential to do this. This could be your story.

Part 2: The Journey

2. The Idea

The idea first came to me during my second year of university as I was beginning to explore my options after graduation. Graduation is a strange time of life because suddenly you are faced with the question of what is it you going to do for the majority of the next forty years, or at least that's what it feels like! And I, like most graduates, didn't really have the faintest idea about what I was going to be doing at the weekend, let alone for the rest of my working life.

Unfortunately, for those of you who are waiting for a step-by-step guide to your ground-breaking idea, this is not the book for you. I don't think any book could do that and even if it did, I'd challenge you to work it out for yourself. If I'm really honest, the idea came to me one afternoon when I was procrastinating from doing my coursework. I was sat there thinking about my future career, my thoughts turned to business and I loved how great the idea of being your own boss sounded. So, in my own self-edifying kind of way, I decided maybe I didn't need a job but could work for myself. At first, I'd just earn enough to get by, and then I'd slowly build up my business empire. Day dreaming can be dangerously influential.

The issue that instantly gripped me was where would the initial investment to begin a venture like this come from? Again, in a strangely anti-establishment thought-process, I decided I didn't need a big investment but could, of course, start a business from something as small as £100, or £10, or maybe even just £1. The idea was born.

At that time, it was just a bit of daydreaming, successfully taking my mind off my coursework for long enough to get me to the next tea break, and fairly quickly, I let it drift to the back of my mind.

That was until a key moment made me take note of the idea again. It was only later that evening when I was walking home from church and I happened to find a £1 coin on the floor. I didn't think too much of it, I picked it up and put it in my pocket. Later that evening it dawned on me that only hours earlier, I had entertained the idea that I could earn my own salary from as little as this very coin. This chance find launched my imagination back into the overdrive of possibility.

The idea was still just a passing personal edification; yet I decided to keep the coin safe in my sock draw, just in case.

So really, it seems you don't even need your own £1 starting investment. You could scour local car parks and high streets and await your future dreams to hit the tarmac.

Before the
journey

3. Before the Journey

I, like most university graduates, had been pulled into the glitz and glamour of the university careers fair. It left me thinking my only option of a fulfilling career would come through securing the Holy Grail... a well-paid grad scheme from a top 100 company.

I applied for a whole range of jobs and succeeded in getting to the final rounds of a handful of appealing grad schemes with high-end companies. Unfortunately, or fortunately, depending on the way you see it, that was where my graduate fairy-tale ended. The best I could do was a deferred entry to one of the schemes; a very good scheme but one that was over subscribed thus forcing a year out before starting. I figured that with some sort of future financial security in the bag, I would have a year out to figure some things out. In the end, I made the decision to give this crazy business idea a go.

When I had finally made the decision to embark on this business adventure, the first thing I did was to tell as many people as I could. It might seem strange to do so, but I had changed my mind about doing it so many times that I was desperate to make it official. Telling so many people gave me an accountability network that I had no choice but to really see it through.

To tell you a little bit about myself, I am a very motivated person and if I set my mind to something I want to achieve I will do everything within my power to make it happen. Having key people in my life now knowing what I was going to do for the next year further motivated me to really push on and make sure it was going to be a year incredibly well spent, and not wasted on a coasting year out. I wanted to surpass their expectations and justify my decision.

Probably the most significant moment in this decision was telling my Dad. To set some context around my previous life choices; I had deferred my university place to move to North Wales and work as a youth worker for two years, I'd got married at twenty, and I'd bought a house to renovate in my second year of University. Each of those massive life decisions I honestly remember very little about speaking to my Dad about, really. But when it came to outlining my vision for this One Pound Challenge, I clearly remember every part of it. I genuinely did not know how he would respond. Unsure about it all, I decided to explain it in the car on a long drive back from

Scotland. My Dad is not a scary person; in fact he is one of the kindest men I know. But considering I had a wife, a mortgage and I was not the youngest graduate in the job market having already had two gap years, I was about to announce an idea that could probably fail, leaving us totally reliant on my wife's wage. Needless to say, it did not go down too well. This was a huge blow for me, making me seriously reconsider my options. Had it been a glorified daydream? Looking back, however, it turns out this conversation was central to my decision to go ahead with the challenge. After the remaining four hours of the journey home, I had to intentionally articulate my reasons for wanting to really give this thing a go. It developed in me a stable foundation I needed to launch one of the biggest challenges of my life to date.

Thankfully, my Dad very quickly turned into one of my best supporters to the challenge, second only to my incredible wife, Rachel.

Starting the
Journey...

4. Starting the Journey

Before starting the journey into my business adventure I had spent a fair amount of time developing, tweaking and sharing the purpose and plan for the challenge. As mentioned previously the idea for the challenge had come over a year before the launch, back on that fateful day I found the pound coin on the floor. Leading up to starting, I had spent the best part of a year compiling a list of project ideas in a notebook I took everywhere with me. Some of the ideas were good, some were not so good, and others were verging on the ridiculous. But every idea I had thought of went into my little blue notebook ready for the day of investment; that pound coin I kept in my sock draw.

During the final few weeks before the start of the challenge, I was taking my final university exams. My final exam was just two days before the launch of my challenge. As you can imagine this meant my time to prepare was limited, or at least it should have been if I had been more focused on revising rather than procrastinating with plans for the launch.

Thankfully, probably by more luck than judgement, my results were good and I had created a detailed plan of action for my first week to make sure the challenge hit the ground running. Also during this time, I had developed a guide plan for the first month and a very basic idea of what the plan for the rest of the year might look like.

Looking back at my plans for the year, they were way off; even my plans for the first month were not that close to reality. Nonetheless, having something in place gave me a good sense of direction and a confidence that the year could work if I worked hard and always had something to keep going. Later in my year when things became really tough and I questioned it all, looking back over these very early plans turned out to be invaluable in reminding me of that original motivation and became instrumental in pushing me on to aim higher.

The One Pound Challenge
2013-2014 -- one man, one pound, one year, whole time

£1

Month 1

5. Lift off: Month One

Month starting total: £1

Month ending total: £1,212

Total net profit: £1,211

We have lift off.

At 8am on the 1st June 2013 I embarked on the first step of my year long adventure. My first investment was washing up liquid. To take my first few jobs I washed up piles of dishes for students who were still sitting their exams. By the end of the first morning and a few piles of clean dishes later, I had earned enough to make an early reinvestment buying some car washing suds. That same afternoon, after more dish washing and car cleaning, I reinvested again expanding my cleaning ventures to house cleaning products. The end of day one.

The first few days were very much based on the good will of local friends who were very generous, putting their name down early to support the launch of my challenge and offering to chuck in some money to have some cleaning done. By the end of the first week, I had cleaned a range of houses, cars and dishes. And without any accidents either, which was fortunate as I certainly could not afford to invest in business insurance so early in the challenge.

The second week continued in much the same fashion as the first, with cleaning and car washing taking the majority of my time. A few new jobs started to offer themselves with gardening and a decorating job keeping me pretty busy and most importantly, that pound investment was growing.

By week 3 I had exhausted most of my local contacts and the kind offerings to clean began to slow down leaving me for the first time with the difficult reality of a day without any work. This was the first difficult obstacle I had to overcome as my early enthusiasm and unashamed confidence that work would keep rolling in had took a hit earlier than I had expected. Consequently, this bought the early launch of my planned pase two.

Phase two focused on looking to invest in somewhat longer return items, such as items to buy in bulk and sell individually on online platforms such as eBay. I also began to pursue other quick-win projects I had previously thought of to continue the momentum, these included; mystery shopping assignments, completing surveys online for cash and developing what turned out to be a very important link to a selection of student landlords across Loughborough.

Towards the end of the first month a key relationship with a large student landlord began to develop opening a vast assortment of moneymaking opportunities. At first the landlord provided the odd job to see how I did, and after working quickly and to the best of my ability, especially when being paid by the hour, the odd jobs soon turned into a regular occasion with lots of cleaning and furniture-building tasks. It provided a steady stream of income and it has started from nothing.

What's more, in the final week of June, I was fortunate enough to be offered a short-term cleaning contract for an office in Loughborough due to their regular cleaner being on leave for a month. This also led to a very lucrative one-off IKEA furniture collection and building service, bringing in the best day of my challenge so far and earning over £220 on that one day alone.

The highlight of this first month was developing working relationships with both student landlords and local businesses. The major thing here was to work to the best of my ability at all times, even if being paid by the hour, as to make those important first impressions with your working ethic and standards. Even when it's a hard and gruelling task, especially on the menial tasks, remember to make good impressions because this will more often than not lead to future work as a trust and respect is built up with them.

The first month gave me a lot of encouragement, from the bottom of every bucket and sink of dirty water. I learnt the true reality of working hard even on the tedious or lowly tasks, knowing it is all building for the future. I also learned to put myself out there and not be afraid of rejection; this is often how an opportunity will present itself.

Month
2

6. Light Bulbs and Lawn Mowers: Month Two

Month starting total: £1,212

Month ending total: £2,891

Total net profit: £1,679

Month 2 came around very quickly. I had spent so much of my first month cleaning and it had worked well, so, I figured, why fix what isn't broken?

The month consisted of plenty more cleaning, car washing, furniture building, decorating, DIY and gardening. It was keeping me suitably busy for most of the month.

The once one-off jobs with student landlords had now hit overdrive and I was working at least 3 or 4 days a week within the student property industry. Best of all, word began to spread across their networks about my business challenge and I was receiving regular emails and phone calls offering more work from new landlords who had a house that needed cleaning work before new students were to move in. Possibly one of the strangest jobs I completed in this time was changing 800 spotlight bulbs over two days for a student landlord; a very repetitive job as I'm sure you can imagine.

Throughout this month I received lots of support from my steadily growing following. The biggest honour was a job offer from a student house agency. I knew I had to respectfully decline and focus on the remaining 10 months of the challenge ahead of me, but it did lead to plenty of freelance work.

Month 2 also saw me commissioned for my first woodworking project for a designer in Loughborough, another project that again would turn into an important part of my year.

Throughout July I had work that kept me busy most days, but on the odd occasion I did have a free day when I would take the opportunity to plan for future projects, look into possible investments with my growing money pot, update social media, and even sometimes just to enjoy a day off and build back my motivation. I soon realised this a great part of working for yourself!

7. Raising the Stakes: Month Three

Month starting total: £2,891

Month ending total: £4,143

Total net profit: £1,252

August saw a shift to a new phase of the One Pound Challenge. It was a move towards a more traditional business as my investment figure reached a more substantial level.

The aim for this month was to begin developing a chain of small businesses that would hopefully make a move away from time equalling money to a more regular income from some intelligent investments. In other words, with the challenge moving into new territory, the stakes had been raised.

Work for student landlords still continued and I had a handful of gardening projects that each took a few days to keep the total growing. I never wanted to turn down an opportunity to work.

The biggest move came as I began selling wholesale items online. I started by testing a variety of items that would guide my upcoming larger investments, while giving a good cash boost for a smaller time investment.

August, overall, was a slightly quieter month with holiday season meaning potential clients were away so I took some time off myself to visit family, leaving work at home so as to spend quality time with them and be fully present.

This break came at a perfect time for me. Starting your own business, especially jumping in headfirst like I'd done is tiring. You need to make sure to take time off, even though everything in you feels the need to plough on through a lack of energy. It feels like stopping might slow the momentum and close potentially open doors. I finally realised the challenge would still be there when I came back from a week off, so I left it in the office (or in my case, my front room) and relax, recover and get my energy levels back ready to advance forward with an even greater enthusiasm than I'd ever had before.

The rest is very rarely in vein. And for me, September turned out to be a cracker.

month
4

8. Selling to the World: Month Four

Month starting total: £4,143

Month ending total: £7,020

Total net profit: £2,877

This point was now a third of the way through the adventure.

So far, there'd been lots of hard work, fleeting time, intense strategizing and planning, plenty of risk-taking and even a fair bit of luck leading to my £1 investment now ringing to the tune of a £7000 investment.

I remember how quickly the first four months had flown by, and yet so much had happened since that first day I was stood in Aldi investing my £1 into a bottle of washing up liquid.

September was a mixed month for me. It had been a month of great increase for the total and still provided plenty of space to dream, think and plan for the challenge's next steps. There had certainly been more of a tangible business management structure to my day with online sales of a selection of items being my major income, as larger and larger investments were made to purchase more stock to increase revenue as far as possible.

However, September had in some ways been a difficult month with the planning of projects not quite lining up or looking like the profitable options they once seemed in the early planning stages. This made me put them on the back burner for a while as I pursued other ideas.

I found I was working from home much more which can be a lonely way to work and at times made me feel a bit lazy, especially as my wife Rachel headed out to work at 7am when I sat leisurely eating my breakfast. I was still regularly working 12-hour days.

September, like much of my challenge, consisted of more planning and research into a selection of business ideas, with a big focus on developing my bespoke woodcarving commission business Radbourne Carving, ready for a launch in October for what I hoped would be a Christmas gift sales rush.

I still did have a number of other projects running, such as gardening and cleaning, and I'd made my biggest single investment to date buying a car to sell on for a little profit; a risky move.

With £1 to £7,000 in four months, things were looking good for the One Pound Challenge; but I needed to keep the momentum going through to Christmas.

Month 5

9. Foraging in Autumn: Month Five

Month starting total: £7,020

Month ending total: £8,966

Total net profit: £1,946

October was another interesting month for me. Autumn had fully taken over with the weather becoming colder and the nights drawing in, adding to the challenge of keeping self-motivated to get up early each morning and have a productive day whilst working mostly from home.

This was the first month where I began to question if I was actually enjoying the challenge. There is an odd pressure that comes from setting up your own business, especially when you are based at home, because the boundaries between work and rest can become easily blurred. Along side that; a constant question of how to work becomes a necessity in your day-to-day life to even just survive financially.

Projects during month five continued much the same way as previous months with the most time being given to continued selling online, which by this time was down to a selective few stock items, mostly cycling jerseys.

My top tip for selling items online is to stick to selling items you understand and would be interested in purchasing yourself; if someone else can sell them in bulk for a profit, why can't you if you find the right supplier?

Also, during month 5, I did manage to sell the car I had bought the month before on a crazy whim investment for a profit of about £500. Additionally, I foraged the hedgerows and made homemade jams and chutneys to sell. It did not create a huge profit here but I had the time and it was good fun to do anyway. There were still a couple of odd jobs I was given including a garden clearance, cleaning and some mystery shopping assignments. Finally, my woodcarving website was launched and various items were created ready for sale on websites such as Etsy, all in the continued hope for plenty of Christmas sales during November.

Month 6

Half way
Point.

10. Half Way Point: Month Six

Month starting total: £8,966

Month ending total: £10,303

Total net profit: £1,357

Month 6 brought me to the halfway point and the £10,000 mark.

Being November, I was attempting to cash in on the inevitable Christmas present-buying frenzy. I promoted my woodcarving business as much as possible with Christmas gifts. In short, it went quite well, but could have been a lot better to be honest. Nothing was lost but I'd hoped for more.

Online sales again were continually bringing in money but. I had begun to come up against a couple of supply issues that meant I had a few days without any stock remaining and it was very frustrating. Unfortunately, this issue continued to happen and it escalated over the coming few weeks leading to a change in direction for the challenge. I'll explain further in the next chapter.

The biggest highlight for November was a day spent walking in the countryside reflecting on the challenge to date and how to move forward. There is something really important when you are on a challenging journey to take time out to reflect and be refreshed. For me, being a farmer's son and a geography graduate, this is getting out in to the natural world. During this time walking, I was able to gather my thoughts, reflecting on lessons from past mistakes and tips to move forward from the good parts. This gave me the personal encouragement to keep going and push on with my challenge as I crested the halfway marker and began my push descent to the finish. As I walked in the crisp fresh air, new ideas began to form for the next stages of the challenge providing an excited motivation for the last couple of working weeks before Christmas.

Overall, November was a fairly good month but I had hoped to earn more during this time. However, breaking the £10,000 marker within the first six months was something to be celebrated and thankful for, my disappointment then was quickly brushed under the carpet and a readiness for some well-earned time off over Christmas was building.

11. Lone Wolf: Month Seven

Month starting total: £10,303

Month ending total: £11,760

Total net profit: £1,457

December was a quieter month for me. I had some freelance work for a local business and I fulfilled all the remaining Radbourne Carving Christmas orders. Then I took all of the Christmas period off to relax and spend time with family.

However, it was not all-festive cheer for me during December. Being over halfway and the end of my year long challenge rapidly approaching, my thoughts started to turn to the future and what I would be doing after this business adventure.

At first my thoughts were to apply for a graduate scheme in business, as surely this business adventure would set me out as a prime candidate for some top employers. It turns out that if anything the challenge actually highlighted me as somewhat of a 'lone wolf' persona (I genuinely received this feedback from more than one employer). They were concerned I would want to do things my way too much for the type of job that required you to fit their graduate scheme mould. Looking back, it was probably a fair assessment, although at the time the rejection really did hurt.

I potentially had another couple of options that I was looking to pursue with work after the year long challenge. These other options continued to slowly process over the next couple of months, and I will unpack them further in the coming chapters.

As for the One Pound Challenge, the coming New Year brought a fresh enthusiasm to push forward and break some new ground for the last half. At the time I hoped to finally move completely away from what had become the bane of my life – cleaning – and instead to extend my activities into some exciting new adventures and projects.

12. Critical Issues: Month Eight

Month starting total: £11,760

Month ending total: £13,490

Total net profit: £1,730

Happy New Year!

The One Pound Challenge business adventure now entered January 2014 and it came with a massive shift in direction.

Supplier issues that I mentioned previously had hit critical levels and I took the decision with the New Year to stop selling online. Instead I decided to push myself to find new working opportunities and started to launch some of the more risky projects I had been putting on the back burner.

However, upon making this decision, a surprise came from the offer of a freelance contract for a month with a business I had been working with before Christmas. This was not only a big encouragement because they were very pleased with the results I was bringing to their growing website (previously studenthouses.com, now called 'Student Crowd'), but it also allowed me to work in an office full of people for a while. This was much better for my state of mind than continuing alone at home in the cold short days of winter. Furthermore, working for this growing business gave me a brilliant insight into a tech start-up business that had investment behind it, this experience taught me so much about business structure, marketing and time-saving tools, which I'd never truly understood.

This freelance contract was full-time hours throughout January and so not a lot else really took place. And you might be pleased to know that January was the first month I did not do any cleaning jobs.

13. February Flying By: Month Nine

Month starting total: £13,490

Month ending total: £14,598

Total net profit: £1,108

February flew by so quickly!

I was offered another months work with the tech start-up business studenthouses.com. Although it was a tough decision to give such a lot of time in the One Pound Challenge to this single freelance project, I accepted because I was learning so much about small businesses and tech start-ups. Plus, being so heavily involved in developing their client base and website, I figured it was right that I stayed for some more time to see tasks through to a fuller completion.

In theory, during this month I was supposed to spend time planning for future projects in the evenings and weekends, but this is was much more difficult than expected. When you leave from a full days work to walk home in the cold and dark, even though it is only 6pm, the last thing I wanted to do is strategize for future projects that seemed far off. This challenge of time investment and motivation brought a realisation that working full time, continuing other projects and trying to have a social life, is a very difficult balance without burning out. How people do all of this and have children to look after as well, I do not know. Unfortunately, this would come back to bite me very soon.

Now with three months remaining, March brought a better rhythm to my time investment.

Month
10

14. Mishaps, Melancholy and Madness: Month Ten

Month starting total: £14,598

Month ending total: £15,321

Total net profit: £723

Oh dear, oh dear, oh dear.

The start of March was, by far, the toughest part of the One Pound Challenge with the smallest rise in my total to date, even smaller than when I was just starting with £1. That was a hard reality to live with.

The difficulty came from not being prepared with new projects when my contract with studenthouses.com came to an end. I found myself scratching my head for the first couple of weeks for ideas of what to do next, reaching a point where I was genuinely unsure where my next pound would come from, never mind my next thousand pounds.

The issue stemmed from the very nature of my challenge being time-constrained. I was trying to see what I could achieve in one year from my pound, which meant I had to prioritise the projects which would provide me with a quick return for my investment, unfortunately these can be quite hard to come by. Then again, if they were easy then I suppose everyone would be doing them. A number of previous project ideas that I'd highlighted as possibilities would not fall within the right time frame for a healthy return within two months.

Just to add further disillusionment, during this time I had not been successful in another couple of job applications and my options appeared to be getting more limited by the week. This was made all the more difficult with the reality that I had not developed a sustainable business option to pursue beyond the end of my year, mostly due to the focus of a return within the year time frame.

Looking back at this time is where my major criticism for the challenge would come. If it was not time-constrained, then March could have been a great opportunity for a larger sustainable business idea with £15,000 to invest.

Thankfully, although close, this is not where my challenge came to an ungraceful end. As if by surprise, I had to remember I had the best part of £15,000 to invest, so why was I just sitting on it?

I braced myself to take a chance with the money I had and invest it on a range of projects that may or may not provide a return, as surely it would be better to end the year on less than I currently had than to not give it an opportunity to grow into more. It was a challenge after all.

With this fresh wave of confidence I stepped out and bought some old furniture to renovate and my most risky investment of all – a Mazda Bongo van.

The final two months were shaping up to be either an exciting finale or a disappointing failure.

15. Campervans and Puppies: Month Eleven

Month starting total: £15,321

Month ending total: £16,478

Total net profit: £1,157

11 eventful months after beginning my business adventure with just a £1 investment and a mission to earn my first graduate salary, there was now just one month remaining!

My total was developing very nicely with investments still to play out. I had to try and learn to not get frustrated with slow repayment investments, all I could do was hope they would make the final month an exciting conclusion to the challenge.

It was April and it was divided suitably into two with a short Easter break in the middle where I took a final bit of time off to replenish before charging for the finish line.

Month 11 consisted of continuing to invest in as much as possible that would hopefully give me some return before my challenge concluded.

My main focus for the penultimate month was to work hard converting the Mazda Bongo van I had purchased into a fully functioning campervan. I knew this project had a great potential to earn a big profit having spent quite a bit of time in the past researching campervans for my personal use, finding that there was a vast price range between the van and converted campervan models, especially during spring when people are planning their summer camping holidays. It was obviously a risky investment as I am not a mechanic and so any issues in this area could have ended in a large financial hit. However, after a bit of time searching for the best deal I found a van that was perfect for me to take a punt on. After a very nervous train journey carrying more cash than I had ever held, I purchased the van and got it home ready to remove the back seats and begin the camper conversion, adding a fold out bed, hob cooker, storage units, vinyl flooring and a lick of paint inside. It took me about 4 weeks to finish the conversion and I have to say I was very impressed with what I had created.

Alongside the camper conversion, the furniture I had bought was beginning to take shape, turning from run down old cabinets no one wanted, to desirable modern shabby chic units.

This was not all; month 11 saw the return of the old faithful cleaning jobs, with a regular office contract taken on. I was happy to receive a few woodcarving orders to keep that project ticking over and I had another good day collecting and building IKEA furniture for an office expansion.

The biggest new project was working with a procurement company called Fersk to launch, develop and gain a better understanding of the long-term potential for expansion of their procurement services in the solar panel industry. This freelance project came with flexible hours to suit me continuing with other on-going projects.

On a more personal note, in April we had a new addition to our household with a new 8-week-old black Labrador puppy called Griff. Or, in other words, I openly invited a very big distraction into our house.

The only thing was to roll on to the finish line and see if I could cash in my investments and finish this year long business adventure as strongly as I had always hoped.

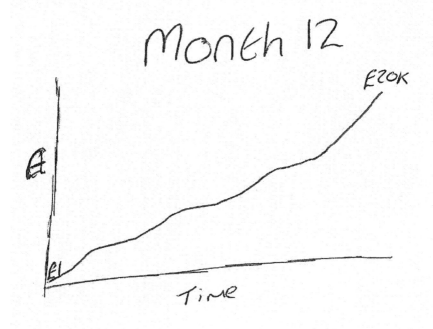

Month 12

£20K

£

£1

Time

16. Final Total Panic: Month Twelve

Month starting total: £16,478

Month ending total: £20,025

Total net profit: £3,547

This was the final push to cash out my active projects and find as many jobs as possible to bring up my total.

Within the first couple of weeks I successfully sold the furniture I had renovated for a small profit and continued the office cleaning contract and freelance work with Fersk. I managed to clear out all the remaining stock left over from past projects and most importantly I had finished and sold the Bongo campervan; it looked great if I do say so myself.

In fact, the campervan sale very nearly didn't happen at all, and not because of a lack of interest but because I really wanted to keep it myself. However the challenge once again had to come first and the sale was a great success, generating about £1,300 profit.

Now, with two weeks to go, a small (!) panic began to set in. I was going to come up short of the £20,000 mark by all of a couple of hundred pounds unless I did something about it. So, I hit social media again searching for those illusive extra jobs gardening or cleaning that would make all the difference. Who wants to hear about the guy who turned £1 into £19,700?

Thankfully some of my previous networks pulled through and provided cleaning and gardening jobs to make my last couple of weeks busy.

And here it is, a year after starting this audacious business adventure with just a £1 investment, having developed a variety of small business projects, working hard and reinvesting, I am very pleased to say my total figure did reach a little over £20,000!

Looking back over my business adventure it is interesting to see how my investment did grow. To be honest, I did not know what would have been possible in a year. I just made sure I kept taking every opportunity that I could based on the current situation I found myself in. With hindsight, I would now know what I would have avoided and what I would have pursued further but that is all part of the adventure that makes the story of a £1 investment growing to over £20k.

During the twelve month journey I developed: a turnover of around £38,500, approximately 100 different job opportunities, 220+ Facebook page likes, 1000+ twitter followers, 42 blogs with 6000+ hits, 28 video's with 1000+ views and a website with 7000+ hits.

To achieve all of this from a lucky stumble across a £1 coin on the floor is quite something, don't you think?

After the Journey

FINISH

17. After the Journey

After finishing my year long challenge I continued to keep myself busy with a variety of projects and on-going contracts birthed from my challenge. This kept a good steady income for a couple of months until I slowly brought all projects to a halt giving myself the summer off to spend some quality time with my wife – Rachel's a school teacher and so has great summer holidays that I wanted to make the most of with her.

Also, during this time I began to look into a range of other project ideas I had kept on hold until I finished my year, as they were not quick return opportunities. Some of these ideas, after much previous excitement, were proven to not be worth the paper they were written on anyway and I quickly dumped them. Some showed early promise but produced barriers that, at the time, I did not have the energy to overcome and so have been placed in the 'maybe one day pile'. Other ideas still have stayed as just early stage ideas for now. So perhaps you should keep an eye out for some exciting things to come in the future.

I think this post-year continuation concludes an entrepreneur's journey appropriately. A lot of the time the ideas you have had in the past that seemed world-conquering turn out to be not so great, whether due to time barriers or misplaced optimism. Of course, not all your ideas will be that bad, however, all of them will almost certainly need tweaking or redefining somewhere along the line. Let it be an encouragement to keep thinking of new opportunities no matter how crazy they may first seem. Keep testing the ideas with thorough planning and strategy development as failure will inevitably happen, it has to, but this never means the end of your journey. Believe me, I've been there and bought the T-shirt.

Personally, my next steps are actually going to be heading back to Loughborough University to begin a PhD in Physical Geography. This is a very different direction, I know, but after thoroughly enjoying and achieving my undergraduate degree, it has always been of interest to me and having the opportunity arise I knew I had to take it. Entering student life again for another three year with self-led time, research and student discount does actually sound quite appealing to me!

As I write this chapter in September 2014, just one month to go before I start my PhD, I am still keeping myself busy.

Mostly, I am spending an inordinate amount of time in coffee shops trying to discover my inner author to write this book you are currently reading.

As for the One Pound Challenge going forward, I hope to continue developing a legacy for my journey that will inspire all those who hear about it.

The One Pound Challenge Legacy

18. The One Pound Challenge Legacy

This business adventure was always going to be more than just for me earning some money and avoiding having to get a 'real job'. I wanted to inspire people who are struggling for money, I wanted everyone to know that there are options out there to earn some extra cash to avoid going into what may seem inevitable or common debt. I wanted to encourage those who want to start their own business that it is not the end of their dream if they cannot get a loan. In fact, there are other more rewarding ways to get your business off the ground without a vast capital investment. I hope that those who followed my journey would agree that I have achieved some of these ideas and that they have indeed been inspired.

But I do not want to stop there. I believe that the journey I have been on through graduation, setting up my own business and having to manage my personal finance incredibly well to get by can inspire and equip others. I believe the story of the One Pound Challenge will become more than an interesting dinner party conversation about a guy who turned £1 into £20,000, I'd love to see it create a legacy of new inspiring stories of how others have stepped out into their own adventure having been encouraged by hearing my story.

The One Pound Challenge legacy comes in a couple of steps.

- Firstly, this book is a great way to share the story of my journey.
- Secondly, I aim to share my story further through taking every opportunity I can to speak about my business adventure, whether this is at entrepreneurial events, business team training sessions, in schools or with a stranger in a shop queue.
- Thirdly, I invite you to connect with me on social media, especially if you have a success story of your own that has been influenced by from hearing about my challenge in any way.
- Finally, please help me grow the reach of my journey by sharing the story with the people you know.

My dream is that if ever I create another edition of this book, I can fill large sections with stories of inspirational people who have gained the encouragement to embark on their own adventures.

Visit to

CAP UK

Bradford

Loughborough

19. CAPuk Visit

Part of the idea behind the One Pound Challenge is to inform people about the different support that is available in the UK for financial education and management. A highlight during my challenge was my visit to the charity CAPuk in Bradford. Read about my experience as it happened:

This week I have been to visit the charity CAPuk at their head office in Bradford.

After attending one of their Money Course Coach training events earlier in the year I was already familiar with their mission. Also, in preparation I'd also just finished reading the story about CAP in John Kirkby's book *Nevertheless* on holiday last week.

Upon arriving at CAPuk Headquarters I didn't know what to expect. Was it still the small operation I had read about in 2006 that was struggling for finance but determined to grow? What had happened since then?

I arrived at mid-morning to the impressive Jubilee Mill building, seeing the distinctive green CAP logo. Ed Parker, the Manager of Capuk Money Course, very kindly took me on a tour around the building. The first thing that struck me was the sheer size and professionalism of the charity. Back in just 2006 CAP was new to Jubilee Mill with a handful of staff. Now, they have around 250 staff members that fill every floor of the massive Jubilee Mill building. The next impression to strike me was the impressive culture. Even a quick tour showed me how infectious their passion is and driving forward with one purpose: to help people break free from crippling debt.

The tour continued and I was taken around the multitude of teams that ensure CAPuk is one of, if not the, best debt crisis support service in the UK. From the initial contact team who receive over 120 phone calls a day, to the set up team who work in conjunction with a local debt centre to begin the management process, the creditor relations team who try to negotiate on behalf of the client for reduced repayments, and through to the repayments team who provide an individual service to ensure their clients become debt free within an agreed timescale, this process is truly remarkable and produces undeniably incredible results. And most astonishingly it is a completely free service! For each team I received an in-depth explanation and they could offer countless stories and statistics of how lives had been changed through the debt crisis service they provide.

Amongst all the incredible stories, it is hard not to notice the passion Ed (and the whole staff team) has for CAP. This is an amazing example of leadership; developing a working culture to ensure all members of staff value and drive forward the vision and mission of the charity, especially during such a time of expansive growth. It really highlights the power a charity can have with the right purpose driven with the highest professionalism.

And CAP is not done yet. They currently have 233 debt centres across the UK providing face to face support for people in unmanageable debts but are still aiming to have a minimum 500 centres by 2020 so that everyone who requires help across the whole of the UK can have access to this crucial, necessary and life changing support. Furthermore, CAP have launched a free Money Course across the country to help anyone and everyone become better with managing their money, providing simple tools and systems to ensure people do not get into unmanageable debts. I can personally highly recommend this course. They have also recently launched a course called Job Clubs that aims to help people back into employment by giving them steps to raise their employability and confidence in finding and keeping a job.

Before heading home I had the opportunity to meet John Kirkby, the founder and International director (did I mention CAP is now also in Australia, New Zealand and Canada!). It was great to actually meet the man behind the story I'd just read on holiday, the guy who literally laid everything on the line to provide financial support for those who needed it most, putting himself in challenging financial situations in order to provide a free service to help those in need. I was able to chat to him about the One Pound Challenge and more about his story and the massive success of CAP. It was immensely encouraging and inspiring. I was a big fan of CAP before the visit, but I can certainly now say I'm an even bigger fan!

If you would like to know more about the story of CAP I would recommend the book *Nevertheless* by John Kirkby or visit their website at: www.capuk.org.

Being Married to the One Pound Challenge.

20. Being Married to the One Pound Challenge

I would not have been able to do this business adventure without the incredible support of my wife Rachel. She has been my biggest encouragement sharing in each and every one of my successes and failures. Therefore, I thought it was only right to give a chapter of this book to her to give a different perspective on the One Pound Challenge adventure. So Rach, over to you...

The One Pound Challenge was a fantastic year full of hard work, perseverance and unknowns. It was a strange year in many ways with so many transitions and new chapters beginning. It was also the first time during our three years of marriage that we were undertaking completely different adventures. Having had two years working together as youth workers, then studying for our undergraduate degrees we had always been working together on the same projects. However, graduation signalled a fork in the road as I began the Teach First Leadership Development Programme and Alan began his One Pound Challenge Adventure. As a result it was a year of discovering of how to support one another in our respective jobs.

The One Pound Challenge was a long time coming. The idea had been brewing in Alan's mind for a long time, like a seed gradually watered when different business ideas popped into his head. The build up involved lots of planning and the support from family and friends enabling the One Pound Challenge to be a shared adventure, was great and would become invaluable as the year went on. Friends provided lots of work in the early days with cleaning and gardening and our design-gifted friends kindly worked on creating the brand for him. Knowing these people were on board and believed, in Alan's vision for the year reassured me that I wasn't crazy for allowing him to pursue this adventure.

Throughout our marriage, Alan has always had little projects on the go. Whilst most students spend their long summer holidays relaxing and travelling, Alan started a business buying and selling PS3 controllers online. Over that summer he generated over £6000, therefore, the following summer before starting final year we went travelling around Australia and New Zealand (students and their holidays!). Alongside that he was always getting excited at opportunities to save money, whether that be on car insurance, broadband or phone contracts. All these experiences comforted me as he started his challenge because I knew without a doubt that he would be successful; he just couldn't help it. It's the way he is wired.

The most difficult aspect of the year for me was communicating to people about what my husband actually did. 'Well, he, umm...' How much detail should I go into? We didn't really know what he was doing. "A year to make as much money as possible" made him sound greedy and self-assured, and he is neither of those things. After a few pitiful attempts at describing his occupation, I decided I would have to begin to go into detail and paint a picture of what Alan was doing. Some people's responses were amazing, they couldn't believe his courage and wanted to know more and signed up to follow him on Twitter. Others were unsure and without meeting Alan, probably decided I was married to an idealist who sponged off his wife. This was difficult but developed in me a greater admiration for what Alan was doing, despite some people's negative reactions.

The first couple of months confirmed my initial confidence in Alan's ability. Work came in, Alan worked hard and money grew from tens of pounds to hundreds quickly. Most of Alan's customers were very satisfied and high praise was sung often. Apart from the occasional quiet days, Alan was always busy working on anything that was offered from building IKEA furniture to fitting 800 light bulbs in a day.

However, most of the work involved physical labour and often working by himself. For Alan this at first was not too much of an issue being naturally introverted, however, it soon became apparent that he missed working along side people as part of a team. My long working hours as a teacher and part-time student meant I often wasn't home until late with planning or marking still to do in the evening. Our conversations soon became difficult to maintain, consisting mostly of my venting about uncooperative teenagers. Alan was a huge support, yet I realised he didn't need to hear about every child's educational progress in maths. Instead, he just needed the highlights and an opportunity to talk about his day. It was a difficult transition from being students to working full-time on completely different projects. Time became extremely precious, with diaries and calendars becoming essential to organising our weeks. After Christmas we began to develop a rhythm for ensuring we thrived at work but also had plenty of time to invest in our marriage, friendships and our local church.

Amongst all the business plans lay the question "What should he do after the challenge year finished?" He applied for several graduate programmes, gaining interviews with several big companies but nothing came of it in the end. And although he was making money from the challenge, there was no obvious business plan to take forward that would generate enough profit to sustain long-term. Christmas passed and still we were not clear on his future. It became a topic of many date night dinners and walks in the countryside. Finally, in April after all the searching and striving for the perfect job, a fantastic opportunity to begin a PhD landed in his lap. It wasn't what either of us were expecting but provided the flexibility of time to have projects still running alongside.

My hope is that he will continue to find ways to exercise his gifts of wealth creation but to support people in making wise choices when it comes to financial decisions and encouraging others to steward their resources well.

Part 3: Graduation

'What do you
mean I have
to pay
council tax?'

21. What Do You Mean I Have to Pay Council Tax?

Going to university is probably the biggest transition for any young person, right?

You're leaving home, your parents won't be around to cook your dinner or do your washing, plus you have to make new friends and try new hobbies. And worst of all you're actually going to have to make it a personal responsibility to get to at least one of your 9am lectures each week.

But, sorry to break it to you students, I actually think there's a bigger challenge around the corner. It's not going to university, it's what you do when you come out at the other end.

Of course university has its own difficulties and challenges and I'm not undermining them. I do think its pretty easy, however, to develop a sort of graduate arrogance, this feeling of invincibility that you'll make it just as soon as they finally release you out there into the big wide world. Then you remember that for those undergraduate years, a quarter of the year was an extended holiday back at home with the extra affection from Mum whose missed you loads while you've been away studying and partying hard.

But then you graduate and that's that chapter of your life closed. Suddenly you realise the big wide world isn't just for you and your dreams. It's full of people, each one just trying to make it. The reality is that it is competitive and overwhelming. That degree that you've worked hard for sort of pales to insignificance when it comes to a business financial bottom line or a deadline for a customer. The job market suddenly seems over-crowded and everyone is in the same boat; except it's more like a cruise ship. Your education was in your own hands, getting to that lecture was worth so much more then than now. Before it was your fault if you didn't make it, now if you don't make it to work, you're fired.

Oh and did I mention the biggest shock of all… you now have to pay council tax!

Even if the interview was good and you got your first job, it's not all sorted. It's just the beginning. Suddenly you're not surrounded by like-minded students, but people who have been in career mode for a while now and probably won't be up for a spontaneous game of ultimate frisbee over lunch.

I'm not saying all this in doom and gloom. Graduating is still one of the proudest moments you can ever go through, it's an amazing achievement in itself and really does open up a world of opportunity on the other side.

I've realised the key, though, is to be prepared to go through all of these emotions of transition; understanding that one decision does not have to dictate the rest of your life. You still have control over your life and your responsibilities. Most importantly, be ready to realise that the hard work has only just begun.

The
Entitled
Generation

22. The Entitled Generation

I've heard people call my generation an 'entitled generation'.

By this they mean people who believe they 'deserve better', and that it is the fault of other people that they can't or don't have exactly what they want and when they want it.

And I think I agree.

Did you know the UK alone holds 2/3 of the total credit card debt in the European Union? This just highlights how the culture within UK society says you do not need to wait to have that new shiny thing as you can just go ahead and put it on the credit card. It's more worrying that people happily do it all the time.

Isn't it interesting that advertisements, by their very nature, are there to make you believe that the things you currently have are not good enough, but that this new, faster, slicker and more expensive item is what you need and deserve. It puts people down; it makes people lose their contentment and happiness with what they already have. We believe the lie and so, we always want more.

I am far from perfect and definitely cannot cast the first stone when it comes to wanting new stuff. I have been dragged, quite happily, into the societal desire for an iPhone, downloaded all the latest life-enriching apps and then forget I ever relied only on the basic functions of a phone. And yet now I constantly have access to my emails; I can check them just before sleeping and first thing as I wake up. In other words, I can never leave work if I let it be that way. This is probably the same for many of us, and it's really sad.

Last year I graduated from university and as an experience I loved it. But I did really struggle with the inward looking nature of it all. The culture dictates that university is all about you; your degree, your loan, your grades, your freedom, your financial control, your future. Even volunteering comes with a promotion for yourself, 'this will look really good on your CV and boost your future prospects'. Sound familiar? Of course, take the opportunity you have to individually invest into your life and your choices. But although it can be good to have seasons in life where you look inwardly to reflect and make the best of your future, when this becomes all that you do, a habit and a lifestyle, it creates a selfish society that is constantly told it deserves better, deserves more, and deserves it now.

I think the biggest issue that has come from this is that people forget that they might have to work hard for things. In my opinion, there is little more satisfying than a good hard days work where you can physically see progress. I think the more our generation realises what they can achieve with contentment and hard work is far greater than anything achieved by entitlement and indulgence.

If you are approaching graduation, or know someone who is, then remember to live each day with integrity. Take time out before big decisions to think about the real motivation for your decision, trying not to succumb to the feeling of entitlement that could be driving your options.

This is not an easy task. Each day I purposefully have to make the decision to be grateful for where I am and what I have, even if I feel things could or should be better than they are. To get a kick-start, why not do something about it? Each morning think of at least three things you are grateful for and physically speak it out as you pour your morning coffee or write it down. It'll soon change your attitude and you'll have a whole list of things to be grateful for in no time.

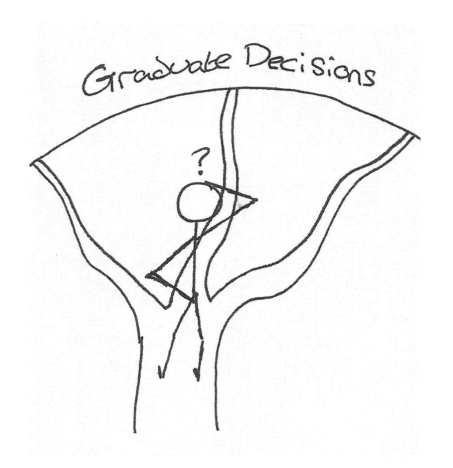

23. Graduate Decisions

Imagine walking along a road and you come to a section that has a choice of three paths. One inclines away right, one drops down left and the other heads straightforward. You have no idea which path to take as you do not know where they lead or want your destination looks like. There is no way of knowing.

What an odd feeling. How can you decide what path to take?

The reality is that this is what life looks like for most graduates. This is a feeling everyone will have at some point in his or her life because as soon as you make one decision another fork in the road will inevitably be around the next corner.

Different people attempt to tackle decisions like this in a variety of ways. Some obsess over each choice, making endless lists of pros and cons in an attempt to strategically make the 'right decision'. Some try to take note of each crossroad decision just in case they end up in the wrong place so they can backtrack to happier times. While others still are blissfully unaware and decide on instinct and power forward to the next decision.

Decisions when you do not know the right answer are difficult. But over this year I have learnt there quite possibly is never a bad choice and more of a sliding scale of good choices. If you stick to your fundamental non-negotiable values and stop agonising over every decision, eventually you will learn to relax and enjoy the journey.

Here are a few tips to surviving graduate life decisions:

1. **Set yourself targets.** At points you can find yourself plodding along and so it's important to remember what you're working towards, especially if you have taken an unconventional route.
2. **Embrace failure** as a valuable experience.
3. **Don't let anyone set limitations over you.** People have their own outlook on life that can often not be too helpful, so don't let that constrain you and remain optimistic through the tough days.
4. **Don't do things alone.** Friends, family and community are key. When you're down they

support you and when you're up they celebrate with you and keep you grounded.

5. **Stay connected to close relationships.** It's natural that you will not keep in touch with everyone you were mates with at uni. It's actually more effort than you think to meet up on a regular basis. Put the effort in though, it's well worth it.

24. Get Started

Graduates (I speak directly to graduates here but this lesson can be applied to any life stage), I have a lesson for you that you probably don't want to hear but I've had to learn it this year and it is really important.

You're not as good as you think you are, so prepare to be humbled!

As a graduate you will find that getting a job can be really tough. There are now thousands of people getting degrees every year and the truth is that there will always be someone who, on paper, is better than you having higher grades, more experience or superior interview techniques.

However, you can turn the tides on this super breed of graduate competition by doing something that will turn your CV from one *of* a million to one *in* a million!

Do something good, different or brave and get yourself hired.

Now entrepreneurship may not sound like an option for you. This is ok. There are whole range of things you can do to make yourself stand out. Volunteer, get involved with a society, and get a part-time job. Whatever you do, don't let your time at university pass you by without investing in something that will make you stand out at least a little. The real key with this, however, is how you portray the activity to a potential employer as it is not particularly about what you did, and more about how this has taught you key transferable skills for the job. Don't tell them a story of what you have done; explain to them how it has prepared you perfectly to be an ideal colleague.

Maybe you are thinking of doing something a little more daring like I've done through the One Pound Challenge, but are held back by the word entrepreneur as you feel it does not fit right with the person you are. But don't worry – I have never studied business, I have no business qualifications, to be honest, I am the opposite of what the stereotype 'entrepreneur' is about. But there is a rising trend of people starting businesses that turn profits and yet still never think of themselves as entrepreneurs, a lot of them don't even think of them selves as business owners, they are just doing what they love and are getting paid for it.

In other words, go for it. Don't let labels and stereotypes hold you back. Make yourself stand out by doing something good. You do not need to be the cleverest, most inspired, well-read person. Get involved in a local project that can give you some experience, or shed the stigma attached to the word entrepreneur by turning your passion into something you can earn money from. All you need is a touch of confidence and a push to get started.

Part 4: Life & Money

25. Managing Money Well

Money, money, money!

For a lot of people it can be a one of the most confusing and scary parts of life. It comes in and out of your account so quickly that if it is not written down, it soon becomes almost impossible to track.

Did you know 61% of people in the UK feel financially insecure? (Source: Uswitch, 2010).

This is probably not breaking news for you. The phrase 'in this economic climate' is being used to describe everything from inflation rates, employment prospects, the housing market and even the price of a chocolate Freddo bar! But will this always be the case of how it all works? Could we make the most of the finances we do have in whatever the economic climate?

The answer is to get in control and keep in control of your money. "How?" you probably ask. The answer is simple and you've probably heard it all before but it's called budgeting.

People quite often think building a budget is hard and complicated or that it means you can't enjoy your money. But this really is not the case if it is done properly. It will control the wasted spending, giving you an understanding of what you do have, allowing for less worrying and more enjoying what you have.

How do I build a budget

A budget is best built for a whole year at a time. To start, you list all of your income (work, student loan, rental income, etc.) and then list all of your outgoings (giving, rent, mortgage, bills, insurance, food, car maintenance, etc.). Try to be as accurate and realistic as possible with your figures by looking at past bills and receipts, this will make it much easier to work out further down the line. Also, remember at this stage to think through your whole year for outgoings on a weekly, monthly and annual scale. Now add them all up and see if it balances (i.e. your incoming money is bigger than your outgoing money).

Now for the balancing act. Maybe you have been fortunate enough to have some money spare. Great. But this does not mean you should blow the rest of your cash on anything. Think about adding some savings or giving to your outgoings, or just budget your remaining money into a fun pot of money so you have a certain amount you know you can spend and then do not overspend thinking you had more.

Or, in the case of many who first budget, it might not balance up. First of all, do not panic. All you have to do is begin to make small changes to get it to balance. You could look to increasing your income or an easier option may be to decrease your outgoings by cutting costs (doing stuff cheaper), cutting back (doing stuff less), or cutting out altogether (just stop doing it). Look through your budget and see how you can do these things to make your income and outgoing balance.

It may be difficult, at first, to get your budget to balance and you may have to make some sacrifices you don't want to make. But when you think longer term about the freedom and responsibility without having to worry about money, it will certainly be well worth it – I promise!

3 Steps to Maintaining Your Budget

1.   Use Cash!

This may be a new (or a very old) concept to you and may seem impractical and old-fashioned, but using cash to pay for things is actually very beneficial. Basically all you need to do is take out the amount you have budgeted for in cash (say £50 a week) and then don't use your card to pay for anything else. I started to use only cash a little while back and was amazed how much easier it is to stick within budget as you see exactly what you spend and how much you have left each week in your budget. Like many others, I have found you do actually end up spending less because you can't spend into next week's budget.

2. **Set up different savings accounts**

Separate out your different pots of money (e.g. weekly living costs, direct debits, annual bills) into different accounts so that when your pay cheque comes in each month you can move the money you need into specific pots. This will mean when the time does come when you need the extra money, it will be there in the account but you're not able to spend it away everyday. This step does take a bit of time and organisation, but it is very easy to set up an account, especially an e-savings account linked to your online banking. In the long run it will be beneficial as you will not have to worry about that upcoming car tax or insurance bill as it will have been budgeted for and built up over time or it's been sitting in the account waiting for you. Student Note: if you get your loan money in lump sums set up an extra account to put it all in and then drip feed the money back into your other accounts each month, treating it like a salary.

3. Keep track of your cash flow

This system of budgeting is great, but you may need to keep an eye on your cash flow to make sure it runs smoothly, especially at the start. I am sure, like me, everything breaks at the wrong time and all the bills come in at once. In times like this, cash flow may be low and so you worry the system is not working. But do not worry, if you have covered all the bases in your budget and you maintain it throughout the year, it will all balance and the time of paying out a lot will be followed by a time of more income. If you really are struggling with cash flow each month, maybe look into changing your bill dates to spread out the expenses, usually companies are more than happy to do this if you just give them a call.

4. Maintaining with annual events like Christmas...

Christmas time, for many, is a budget-busting nightmare but it definitely does not have to be. Think about how much

Christmas costs early, budget to save for it all year and then stick to it. Treat it the same as the rest of the year's outgoings.

Perhaps you are worried about affording this Christmas because you haven't even thought about budgets before. Do not panic and put it all on credit. Why not be proactive and do something creative to earn it. I started from just £1 and a year later, handover £20,000! It really can be done and makes the spending of it much more enjoyable knowing what you have been through to get there! Besides you'll even have fun getting creative and learning new skills and character along the way.

Maybe you do not have the time to earn extra money. If this is the case, why not have a make and mend Christmas just like someone I met along my journey did (find out more about her journey at http://mymakedoandmendyear.wordpress.com). You do not have to buy everything from new for it to be a special gift. Think about making cards, food gifts and photos – they can be just as special, if not more!

Living within your budget is one of those things that will be difficult at times. But I cannot encourage you enough to hold on and trust that once your budget is set up and you get in the right mind-set to live within it, you will be taking so many steps towards being financially secure, responsible and free.

Saving while living for today.

26. Saving While Living for Today

During my One Pound Challenge I tried to learn how to deal with my distinctive desire to save. I am a massive fan of planning for the future; to be honest sometimes I have to stop myself from daydreaming about what life could be like in ten years time, forgetting to live in the moment, much to my wife's distress.

Yet this is a real issue that I think many people will struggle with. How can you save for the future, pay off your mortgage and give generously all while keeping up with the daily demands on your finances by just living?

It is a tension that can easily cause conflict within yourself or your relationships. My wife and I have recently been creating a budget for this year and realised how far apart in thinking we are. I want to save as much as possible and pour money into paying off our mortgage, happily deciding not to do certain things for a while (possibly to a point of hibernation) so that we can maybe one day reach our dreams for a family home. Whereas she wants to have a bigger events pot of cash to do more things in the now and enjoy life. Which is the best option? Well probably a happy medium needs to be found and fortunately I have an amazing wife so our medium can be found.

I think the key to unlocking this tension for people that are like me is to understand that living in the moment is so important. What fun would the future be if you are financially secure but you have no friends to share it with because you never did anything with them to build those relationships? On the other hand, to those who live carefree financial lives, planning for the future is also important. What use will it be to have all the friends in the world but no finance to do anything with them?

Take some time to sit back and reflect on the hidden tensions you might have in your finance between saving and living in the moment.

Generosity is outdated

Generous

27. Generosity is Outdated

I think to give financially on a regular basis is incredibly important.

To give our money is a great way to keep check of what hold money and possessions are having on our lives. It is far too easy for money to creep in as a silent stressor; controlling our lives by turning our eyes downwards, away from the rest of the world, to our own hands and what is in them. It's a bit like Gollum from *The Lord of the Rings.*

I once heard a great anecdote about money. The flow of money is a bit like a river; it flows in one end and out the other, keeping a natural balance in the process. We can try to dam the river to hold back the flow (in other words, keep money for ourselves), however when we do this the water begins to flood every area behind the dam, clogging up the stream and eventually over time becoming stagnate and poisonous. We should treat money like a river, allowing it to freely flow in and out the other side keeping a natural, clean, life-giving flow.

Do not get me wrong. I also believe saving is important. But I also think that sometimes we need to come to a point where we decide to lower our aspirations for ourselves in order to give in support of others.

I want to go a step further. I think the word generous should be retired. In today's society, the word generous has become diluted. All too often I hear people use the word generous in a washed down kind of way; 'he paid for my cup of tea, how generous', 'she's generous, leaving a 10% tip', 'how generous of you giving me your last *Rolo*'. The word is now one of those things where we have become so blasé about that it does not carry the same meaning.

I want to set down a new challenge for giving. No longer do I want to be a person who is just generous, but I want to be a person who when giving can choose to give audaciously!

To give audaciously is to give through sacrifice. It is not to chuck in spare change to a collection as a token gesture because you feel compelled to but to seriously think on your giving and how this money could really bless someone, thus making you consider your giving beyond your own self but as a life giving honour for the other.

I love the quote; *'You make a living by what you get, but you make a life by what you give.'*

My dream is to see this generation turn from a people who are so preoccupied with what they want or feel they deserve, to a generation who will make a difference to help and support others through really seeing the world around them and understanding the difference they can make if only they took the time to consider a small financial sacrifice.

Would you join me in my journey to find what it means to give audaciously?

The Frustration gap of dreams

28. Frustration Gap of Dreams

Dreaming about the future can be fun. Letting your mind run wild with ideas, plans and outrageous hope can be really good for you.

But all too often people's dreams become smaller and smaller as they grow older. The audacious plans of youth to conquer the world soon become a hopeful plan to just make it to the end of the day on a Friday in one piece.

When I first wrote this chapter I was writing to encourage myself to dream big again (and hopefully inspire others to do the same). During the One Pound Challenge I found that the dreams and expectations I had at the start soon became weakened as reality took over. Now this is not to say I am not pleased with how the challenge went, I did reach my personal secret target, but that is the problem, I only reached the target, I did not surpass it in a blaze of excitement.

I think the issue comes when you have a dream that is not completely fulfilled. There is a thing called the 'frustration gap'. This frustration gap is difficult to swallow, it makes you question your ability and your dream so next time you chase a dream; you lower the aims in the hope that the frustration gap is not quite so big this time. However, often it is. This process continues dream by dream until your big exciting dreams become small and insignificant.

Please do not think I am an entitled young dreamer with my head in the clouds. Dreaming is great; it builds hope for those who need it. It can change lives, families, towns, and even nations. But the best dreamers know how to keep grounded in the reality of their situation. The truth is you are not as good or important as you think you are, you probably will not be the person who singlehandedly eradicates world hunger or becomes the Prime minister. But you could be the person who leads a change in feeding those in need in your town, or providing a safe place for the homeless to sleep, or supporting a family through a difficult time like the pressure of crippling financial debt.

So I am challenging myself, and you, to dream big once again. View your dreams with fresh and hopeful eyes, looking at what could be achieved as a best-case scenario, rather than the worst-case.

Take courage to make the tough decision. This may lead to a painful frustration gap but surely that would be much better to deal with than being haunted by regret.

Write down your original dreams and keep coming back to them so you can continue to dream as big, if not bigger!

now --
future

Strategically tackling
the future.

29. Strategically Tackling the Future

You may have a business you want to start or move onto the next level or you may want to get your finances in control. To do this you need to take the time to strategically plan how it is possible.

At the start of each year, I sit down to reflect over my last year and think ahead to what the next has in store. But to be honest, I find sitting trying to think about a whole year really difficult. My thoughts turn into a confused jumble of expectations, enthusiasm, nerves and uncertainty. Having gone through this multiple times I realised it was pointless to try and visualise a whole year. No one really knows what a year could hold.

Now, instead of thinking, I have begun to set out ways to strategically tackle the next year by following four steps:

1. **Aim:** What is it that fundamentally you want each decision you make throughout the year to be based on?

Set fundamental principles that define you for the year. These are not things that you want to achieve like New Year Resolutions, but more like the fundamentals of what makes you tick. This could be things like spending time with family and friends, giving your time and finance to a charity, or pursuing a deeper understanding of faith.

2. **Plan:** What would you like to achieve throughout the year? And practically how are you going to do this?

Plan in challenges to keep the year fresh and holidays to look forward to. Do you always end up sending birthday cards too late, then why not buy your year supply now so all you have to do is send it when the time comes? These plans can be as big or little as you like.

3. **Budget:** Get your finances in order. Make a budget and stick to it.

Then you will not have the restraint of finance haunting everything you do. Through understanding your budget you will set a cap on your living that will release you to enjoy what you can do rather than pine for something you cannot afford.

4. **Rest:** Make sure you have regular times of rest.

All too often we start a New Year or project wide-eyed and bushy-tailed, striving to achieve a resolution and burn out before we get anywhere near. So rest. Find the place you get revitalised and plan in regular short breaks to do this. This place may be a walk in the woods, playing sport, having a night to just sit and read a good book, or even just a Saturday morning coffee and a paper in your slippers; whatever it is, find it and do it without worrying about what you have got to achieve because if you have completed step two you are planned and on track to achieve your goal.

Hopefully these simple strategies will help you prepare for all that is to come and have a great year. Why don't you now sit down and take fifteen minutes to begin strategically tackling the year ahead?

Part 5: Business

30. Think Smaller

When starting a business most people's first thought is about where the seed capital will come from. This likely leads to a prolonged time spent developing financial projections without having ever traded and putting launch on hold until that rare investor will come on board. Sound familiar?

Personally I think this is a waste of time. Unless you're starting something like a factory or restaurant you do not need cash from elsewhere. I would suggest that outside cash should be a last resort.

The One Pound Challenge started with a £1 investment. A year later I had a little over £20,000 to the business name. Imagine what could happen if you spared £100 and a couple of years to invest in getting your business off the ground?

Firstly, you would be able to launch quickly, beginning to get the name of your company out there and attracting potential clients. Secondly, you will be more agile to deal with refining your business model and service as your operation is growing at a more organic rate. And finally, you will have a greater appreciation for what you are building. Trust me!

Would it be feasible to slowly build up your business while earning the capital you need to fully launch in other ways? This keeps you as the sole owner of your company.

I understand the attraction of a lump sum investment from an outside party; it is nice spending other people's money without piling financial risk upon yourself. But the truth is that outside money makes your growth much more restricted as now you have someone else to answer to.

You may be thinking that your business needs to reach a certain level quicker than organic growth will allow to actually succeed. However, many new companies spend too long focusing on building an expensive infrastructure first, neglecting the key development of the business. Although structure and money seem like the right path forward, it can be very restrictive to developing an agile and successful new business.

Hopefully there will be a time when you have the opportunity to grow bigger to reach the next level, but for now can you do with less? That is the question at hand.

When you first start out in business you will be the smallest you will ever be, making you the most agile to tweak and iron out any teething issues. You should embrace it! Being small at the beginning is a good thing, it allows you to develop a strong base to grow and learn from

Do not be afraid of starting small, testing the market and building a strong base to move forward.

Work Hard!

31. Work Hard

During the One Pound Challenge I completed a series of simple DIY and decorating tasks for a family in Loughborough. I set about the work as I always do, trying my best to complete the best job in a good time. After finishing the work the family were very happy with my work ethic and what I had done and I went on my way, A couple of weeks later I got a call from the gentleman to offer me more work, but this time in a freelance business development role for his business based in Loughborough. Can you believe an ordinary DIY job finished with integrity led to me picking up a variety of contracts that created work for the following five months.

'You can train competence, but not character'

The lesson I learnt from this experience was to work hard at all times with character and integrity. The right people will recognise your hard work and you will know you've done a job to the best of your ability.

This approach to work can be especially hard when you are paid by the hour, as it would be easy to slow your workload to stretch it out and earn more money. Yet I would urge you not to do this. From my experience of setting up my own business, if you work hard from the start in order to impress, it will more often than not lead to future contracts that could even be paid better than before.

Working hard is not easy, that is why it is called hard. At times when motivation can be lacking, you may question the point of your work and even begin to think of ways you can get out of it. But, keep going! The best athletes in the world do not get to do the sport they love because they have outrageously more talent than everyone else. They are successful because they have put in the years of training to get to the point they are at.

In other words, train hard. See tough times as an opportunity to build your character and do not give up, as you never know what is around the next corner.

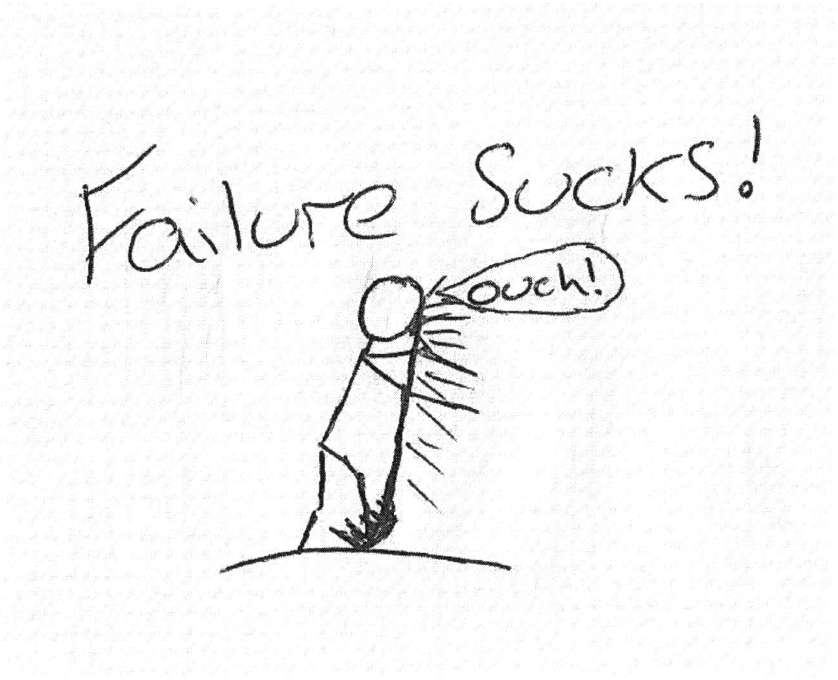
Failure Sucks!
ouch!

32. Failure Sucks… So Get Failing!

We all know it... Failure sucks!

Some business folk say failure is a right of passage. I don't agree. I do not think you have to fail five, six or seven times before you have a successful business, because the truth is that it is inevitable that you will fail on some level; you cannot be perfect from day one. There is no reason why your first business cannot be a success. If you are aware that during the process you will come against some failure, you can prepare for this so as to survive, if not thrive from, the experience as it refocuses your attention and makes you change something for the better.

When I started my year, I don't think I was fully prepared for failure. On quite a few occasions when things went wrong it would really knock me and I would struggle to push on and get motivated again. However, I think was the major learning curve I needed. It prepared me for when I was applying for jobs and got to final stages but never seemed to reach that offer, or times when I was left without work for a while, forcing me to have to be creative with my time and talents.

A really good friend of mine, Caleb Meekins, has been on his own adventure over the last year attempting to face failure head-on by putting himself in forty situations where he will inevitably fail. This social experiment into rejection therapy is called *My 40 Days*. So far it has been a great success, encouraging people not to be afraid of failure, while honestly facing the fact that rejection hurts.

Likewise, an entrepreneurial group based in Loughborough University have set up an event to inspire entrepreneurs and business owners to 'fail forwards'. The premise is to gather together a group of small business owners to share stories of failure and how they have dealt with it, encouraging the network that failure does happen, it hurts, but it is not the end. In fact it can actually make you stronger providing a fresh forward momentum.

Failure sucks... and we all fall short at some point. The key is to know how to pick yourself back up, learn from your mistakes and move on, stronger for it.

Retreat to Advance

33. Retreat to Advance

Owning your own business can make it very difficult to switch off when you're not working. It is natural to have thoughts about how to complete a project or how to move forward running through your mind at all times. However, after just a year of this mind-set, I can see how draining it is, making other areas of your life very strained.

Throughout the year a key principle of my working pattern was to have a time to 'retreat to advance'. This is a time where I intentionally step away from work to reflect on the direction the business is going and to get a fresh perspective on any growing issues.

Within working culture, especially within entrepreneurial circles, there seems to be a sadistic honour in being a workaholic, burning the midnight oil by pulling all-nighters to achieve a self-set goal by a certain time. With this orientation, people try to fix problems by throwing endless hours at the project, attempting to be the hero who sees brute force as a suitable means to create a desired result. However, this drive in attitude is not being a hero, it is merely a mask to cover intellectual laziness.

If you face an issue or a tough decision, the first thing you should do is retreat to a place where you can gain a fresh perspective on the problem. This retreat will allow for a refreshing of the mind to create a strategically time-efficient solution, leading not only to the desirable result within time, but also allowing you to avoid burnout.

Retreating can be done in a variety of ways and is very individual to the person and situation. For example, if I faced a tough direction decision that was going to be vitally important in the progress of the One Pound Challenge I would take as much as a full day out, where I would go out into the countryside and gain my refreshment through connecting with nature (this is the geographer in me coming through). This would give me fresh eyes and motivation for the problem.

For you it could be something as simple as going for a coffee, playing sport, or maybe even getting away for a weekend. Whatever it is find the place that refreshes you and do not be afraid of taking the time to use it.

A business
is like a
fine wine

34. A Business is Like a Fine Wine

Your original, inspirational, ground-breaking, world-changing business will not be an overnight sensation.

Unfortunately, despite popular belief, there really isn't such a thing as an instant hit or overnight millionaire. The truth is the stories you hear about overnight success is just a part of the story. Most of the time when you dig a little deeper, you find that people have been plugging away patiently for years before their idea actually takes off, as we know it.

The rise of Crowd Funding popularity in the last few years has led to many people becoming lazy with their business plans, thinking that it is the luck of the draw for a project to succeed. Therefore a glut of half-hearted attempts for seed capital acquirement has reached crazy levels with some people churning out business ideas in under an hour, just in case that is the idea that takes off.

I think it is important to approach your business growth plans like the creation of a fine wine – slow and steady. Try to aim for slow measured growth; it is hard and you have to be patient, but if you do it for long enough the right people will begin to take notice and get on board. Do not rely on a media rush or crowd funding alone for success, the chances of this happening is little to none.

Do not start with a big PR campaign, but slowly build up your audience alongside developing the best product and service you possibly can.

When I started the One Pound Challenge, I thought that people would take an interest from the start and a huge following would build. It did not. I spent so much of my time trying to share the challenge that sometimes I neglected the point of the challenge, which was to work, hard on growing my pound. That was the eventual story that people would take note of, not how many twitter followers I already had. So a few months in I took the decision to cut back on my media involvement in order to focus on developing the story to tell afterwards, as people want to read a success story, not a year long and slow development, week by week.

The One Pound Challenge is definitely not an overnight success. Not only was it eighteen months in the planning, twelve months in the journey, and now it's getting close to six months after finishing and I'm writing this book, all still with a relatively small and slowly growing audience. But I will keep sharing my journey with every opportunity I get.

Start building your audience today. Get people interested in what you have to say and then keep at it. Then you never know, in a few years, people might be discussing your overnight sensation.

Los Pollos
HERMANOS

Nothing is
'Just Business'

35. Nothing is 'Just Business'

The first rule is: 'nothing is just business'.

If it belittles, undervalues or hurts someone else, it is not right. Live and work with integrity, trying to support and equip others. Do not ever justify something by calling it business!

Over the last year as I have been talking to people who are interested in setting up their own business, one of the biggest reasons for them not going for it was surprisingly not the financial worry, but the fear of the word 'business'. So many people see the business world as a cutthroat industry, scared by the lie that everything is justifiable if it gets you ahead. Many people do not follow their dreams because of this worry.

The thought process that things can be chalked up to being 'just business' in truth is just ridiculous. Do you really think customers will come back to you if they feel let down? Do you think suppliers will be happy to give you a discount in the future if you burn them in a previous interaction? Do you think you will get the best from your colleagues and employees if all you do is undervalue them? Of course you won't.

We need to stop this lie that things are not personal or accountable and 'just business'. Instead, let's begin to clean up the name of business by trading with integrity, building lasting, trustworthy working relationships and honouring and valuing our colleagues.

Part 6: Final Thoughts

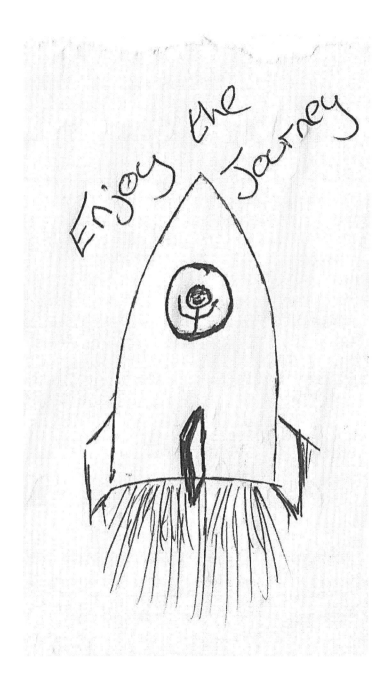

36. Enjoy the Journey

The business adventure I have been on with the One Pound Challenge has been filled with many highs and lows. There were times when I thought I was going to fail and other times when I thought I would conquer the world.

During the challenge my focus to get through a tough time was often on the end goal of seeing what I could achieve with my £1. Yet now I realise that there is so much more richness in the journey than in the final result.

Ernest Hemingway said: *'It is good to have an end to journey towards, but it is the journey that matters in the end'*.

I hope that reading the story about my graduate journey from £1 to £20,000 has inspired you. But most of all I hope my business adventure will encourage you to enjoy the journey you are on, knowing it is not about the end game but what happens along the way.

One Pound Challenge Links

Find out more at:

www.MyOnePoundChallenge.co.uk

Follow the challenge on twitter:

www.twitter.com/pound_challenge

Like the Facebook page:

www.facebook.com/onepoundchallenge

Watch the promotional video here:

https://www.youtube.com/watch?v=0AaJ54HTmqI

10041904R00084

Printed in Great Britain
by Amazon.co.uk, Ltd.,
Marston Gate.